Beaks and Bills

by M.C. Hall

Scott Foresman
is an imprint of

Glenview, Illinois • Boston, Massachusetts • Mesa, Arizona
Shoreview, Minnesota • Upper Saddle River, New Jersey

Photographs
Every effort has been made to secure permission and provide appropriate credit for photographic material. The publisher deeply regrets any omission and pledges to correct errors called to its attention in subsequent editions.

Unless otherwise acknowledged, all photographs are the property of Pearson Education, Inc.

Photo locations denoted as follows: Top (T), Center (C), Bottom (B), Left (L), Right (R), Background (Bkgd)

CVR Getty Images; **1** © James Urbach/SuperStock; **3** Gay Bumgarner/Getty Images; **4** (T) Valueline/Punchstock, (B) (C) © DK Images; **5** Getty Images; **6** Andy Rouse/Getty Images; **7** (T) © Anthony Mercieca/SuperStock, (B) © Purestock/Alamy, (C) STEPHEN ST. JOHN/National Geographic Image Collection, (CR) © James Urbach/SuperStock, (CL) Ben Hall/Getty Images, (BL) © George D. Lepp/Corbis; **8** © Clare Charleson/Alamy Images; **9** Brian Kenney/Getty Images; **10** Getty Images; **11** © Hal Beral/Corbis; **12** Radius Images/Jupiter Images; **14** Getty Images; **15** © Ron Sanford/Corbis

ISBN 13: 978-0-328-39431-9
ISBN 10:   0-328-39431-9

1 2 3 4 5 6 7 8 9 10 V0G1 17 16 15 14 13 12 11 10 09 08

Have you ever watched a robin try to catch a squirmy worm? The robin tugs and tugs until it pulls the worm right out of the ground.

That's how a robin gets its dinner. A robin doesn't have hands and fingers like you do. It doesn't have paws like a squirrel or many other animals. A robin has a beak, or **bill.** Like all birds, the robin uses its bill as a tool to feed itself.

Let's take a closer look at birds and all the things they do with their incredible bills.

Did you ever wonder what a bird's bill is made of? Believe it or not, a bird's bill has something in common with your fingernails and a horse's hooves. All three are made of a **material** called keratin. Keratin is a hard covering that is actually a special layer of skin.

A bird's bill is like your mouth. You use your mouth to eat and to talk and sing. A bird uses its bill the same way. It opens its bill to swallow food and to make sounds and sing songs.

Beaks, fingernails, and horses hooves are made of keratin.

A bird doesn't have teeth like you do. That means birds don't chew their food. Instead of teeth, a bird's bill has small, sharp ridges along the edges. The ridges help the bird hold onto things with its bill.

Did you know that a bird's bill is also its nose? Most birds have holes called nostrils on their bills. Birds use their nostrils to breathe and to sense smells, just like you do.

A bird's nostrils are on the top of its bill, on the end closest to the bird's head.

Birds have bills in all sorts of shapes and sizes. Birds can do all sorts of things with their bills. Many birds use their bills to pick up and carry nesting materials, such as **twigs** and blades of grass. Then they use their bills again as tools to build their nests.

Birds also use their bills to keep themselves clean. They poke around in their feathers with their bills. This helps them find and pick out dirt and tiny insects. They can use their bills to smooth down their feathers and keep themselves neat. Keeping clean helps birds fly.

Keeping its feathers clean is one way this bird stays healthy.

The most important thing a bird uses its bill for is to feed itself. In fact, the size and shape of a bird's bill can tell you a lot about what it eats. Birds' bills have adapted, or changed, over millions of years. Read on to find out how birds' bills are specially designed for the foods they eat.

Can you guess which birds these bills belong to?

Tweet! Tweet! Tweet! A birdfeeder can be a busy and noisy place. Many birds eat the seeds of plants, such as sunflowers, that people put in birdfeeders. However, seeds have hard coverings that protect the seed inside. Before a bird can eat a seed, it has to get through this covering.

That is why birds that eat seeds have short, thick, hard bills. Their bills have a groove inside. The bird picks up the seed and puts it in the groove. Next, it uses its bill to break the covering. After that, the bird takes out the seed with its tongue. Then it spits out the covering. Cardinals, sparrows, and other birds in the finch family are seed-eating birds.

Some birds use their feet to hold a seed while they break open the covering.

Rat-a-tat! Rat-a-tat! A woodpecker bangs its hard, sharp bill against a tree trunk. Then it bangs again and again. What is the woodpecker doing?

It's looking for insects that live under the bark. The woodpecker uses its bill as a drill to make a hole in the tree. Once the hole is big enough, the woodpecker sticks its tongue inside to catch insects.

Some woodpeckers use the holes they drill to store acorns and other nuts to eat later.

A woodpecker's head is very strong. This keeps the bird from getting hurt when it bangs its bill against things.

This hummingbird's wings are moving very fast even while it eats.

Bzzzzzzzz. That buzzing sound isn't coming from a bee. It's the sound of a hummingbird's flapping wings. Do you know why this little bird has such a long, thin bill? It's because a hummingbird's favorite meal is nectar, a liquid that is found inside flowers. The hummingbird's bill is hollow, like a straw. The hummingbird sticks its long bill into the center of a flower. Then it sucks up the nectar.

Nectar isn't the only thing hummingbirds eat. These birds can open their bills like tweezers to grab and eat tiny insects.

Swoosh! An eagle is soaring overhead. It's carrying a fish in its clawed feet. The eagle may be taking the fish to its **platform** nest to feed its young.

Eagles, hawks, and owls are **hunters**. They catch and eat animals such as fish, mice, snakes, and rabbits. These hunting birds all have very sharp, hooked beaks. They use their beaks to tear meat into pieces small enough to swallow.

The eagle is a hunting bird. Can you see its hooked beak?

Splash! A swan is scooping up water in its long bill. What is this bird doing? The swan isn't just getting a drink. It is having its dinner. Swans and many other water birds eat tiny plants and animals that live in the water. They have special bills with ridges that act like a comb. The ridges catch the food and let the water drain out. Then the bird swallows its dinner.

Some ducks and other water birds eat snails and other animals that live at the bottom of ponds and lakes. These birds dive down to scoop up dinner from **tons** of mud and **goo**. Their bills strain out what they don't want to eat.

The swan has a bill that strains the water from its food.

Kerplunk! A big frog hops into the water. A hungry heron waits in shallow water nearby, looking for its dinner. The heron's head moves forward quickly and grabs the frog with its bill.

The heron's straight bill is long and pointed like a spear. It's the perfect tool for grabbing or stabbing fish and frogs.

Herons hunt for their food in shallow water.

Now let's think about the robin again. Does it have a bill specially made for eating worms? Not really. Robins and many other birds have bills that are suited for finding and eating many types of food. A robin eats worms, insects, fruit, and berries. A robin's bill is just right for eating all of these things!

Glossary

bill *n.* the hard mouth part of a bird's body; also called a beak

goo *n.* sticky, wet material

hunters *n.* animals that chase and catch other animals for food

material *n.* what something is made from or used for

platform *n.* a raised, flat surface

tons *n.* a measure of weight. One ton equals 2000 pounds

twigs *n.* small branches of trees or bushes